Contents

Many peoples and cultures

Religion is an essential part of the kaleidoscope which makes up Eastern Europe.

In the West most people take their nationality for granted. However this has not been the case for the people of Eastern Europe. They are from a variety of ethnic groups, but these groups have not formed the basis on which individual countries have been created. Instead, the region has been ruled, over the last 200 years, more or less continuously by dominant empires. In response, the people of Eastern Europe have placed great emphasis on their ethnicity and their religious beliefs to help strengthen their sense of identity.

Ethnic groups

The large area of Eastern Europe contains a variety of people who speak a variety of languages. The Slavs form the largest group. Ethnic Russians, Ukrainians, Poles, Czechs and Slovaks belong to this group. Other groups include the Latvians and Lithuanians, the Estonians, the Romanians, the Hungarians, the Jews and the Gypsies.

▼ A map showing the present-day area of Eastern Europe which, in this book includes Russia (west of the Urals), Ukraine, Belarus, Poland, Romania, Hungary, the more centrally positioned Czech Republic and Slovakia plus the Baltic states. Bulgaria, Albania and the former Yugoslavia have not been included.

Barents Sea

Ural Mountains

Norwegan Sea

Atlantic Ocean

North Sea

Baltic Sea

RUSSIA

ESTONIA

LATVIA

LITHUANIA

RUSSIA

• Moscow

BELARUS

POLAND

CZECH REP.

SLOVAKIA

UKRAINE

MOLDOVA

HUNGARY

ROMANIA

Black Sea

Caspian Sea

From Eastern Europe

Sarah Horrell

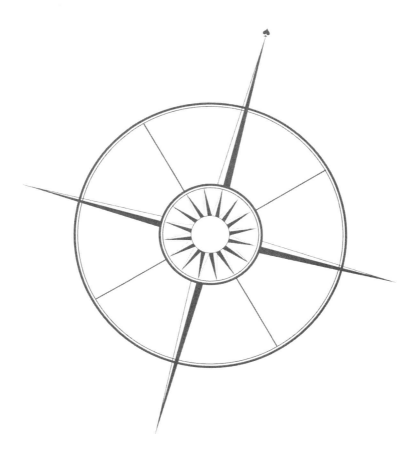

W
FRANKLIN WATTS

Originally published as Origins:
Eastern Europe

This edition first published in 2002
© Franklin Watts 1998, 2002

Franklin Watts
96 Leonard Street, London EC2A 4XD

Franklin Watts Australia
56 O'Riordan Street,
Alexandria, NSW 2015

Editor: Sarah Snashall
Series Editor: Rachel Cooke
Designer: Simon Borrough
Picture Research: Sue Mennell

A CIP catalogue record for this book is
available from the British Library

ISBN 0 7496 4534 2 (pbk)

Dewey Decimal Classification 947

Printed in Malaysia

Picture acknowledgements:
t=top; b=bottom; m=middle; r=right; l=left
AKG London pp. 3, 15r
The Anchorage Museum of History and Art, Alaska
p.8t *Oululuk*, Louis Choris, picture ref. 81.68.7
Bridgeman Art Library pp. 5b *A Religious*
Procession in the Province of Kursk, Ilya Efimovitch
Repin (Private Collection), 6t *Promenade in Tabon,*
Hungary, Miklos Barabas (Magyar, Nemzeti Galeria,
Budapest), 10b *Jewish Scholar in his Study*, Willem
van Nieuwenhoven (Phillips), 12b *Knox Ranch,*
Idaho, (State Historical Society of Colorado, Denver)
Jean-Loup Charmet, Paris pp. 5t (*B.N*),
9(background) (B.N), 18t, 18b
Corbis/Bettman/UPI p.12t
e.t.archive pp. 8b (Historical Museum, Moscow,
Russia), 10t, 16
Mary Evans Picture Library pp. 9(inset), 19l
Eye Ubiqitous pp.19b (Hugh Rooney)
Sonia Halliday pp. 14t (Jane Taylor), 15tl, 22t (Barry
Searle), 23b (Barry Searle)
Hulton Getty Collection pp. 11, 14b, 17b, 20b, 24-25,
26t, 26b, 27b
Hutchison/Haslam p.4
Image Bank/Steve Satushek p.7
Impact Photos/Sally Fear p.13b
David King Collection pp. 6b, 17tl, 17tr, 20t, 21
Performing Arts Library/Clive Barda p.28l
The Polish Library, London 13t
Popperfoto pp.24
Rex pp. 25 (Herbie Knott), 27t (Sipa), 28r (Sipa), 29t
(Sipa), 29b (Sipa)

▲ The different ethnic groups speak a variety of languages. This 19th-century print shows (from left to right) Hungarians, Slavs and Romanians whose languages are all distinct and unrelated.

▼ A religious procession in Russia. Religious processions and festivals are an important feature of the Russian Orthodox church.

Religious differences

Religion is an essential part of the kaleidoscope which makes up Eastern Europe. Christianity arrived in the region at the end of the 10th century and came from two different directions. Monks and missionaries from Rome converted the Western Slavs in the areas that are now Poland and the Czech Republic to Catholicism and the Latin script was adopted. The Eastern Slavs, however, were converted to Christianity by Greek missionaries from Byzantium (now Istanbul), the main centre of early Christianity in the East. This form of Christianity became known as Eastern Orthodox and the Cyrillic alphabet (an alphabet based on the Greek alphabet) was adopted. The other significant religion was Judaism, the religion of the Jewish people.

Three empires

The area of Eastern Europe was divided between three powerful empires. These empires were the Russian Empire, the Austrian Empire and the Ottoman (Turkish) Empire.

The contrast between the lifestyles of the wealthy landowners and those who worked on their estates was very marked.
▲ A family walk around their estate in Hungary.
▼ Russian peasants work in the fields.

Nobles and peasants

The social structures of these empires were remarkably similar: most of the people were peasants who were ruled by small numbers of rich landowners and officials. There was virtually no indigenous (natural to the area) middle class. Instead there was a middle class supplied by people who were themselves originally immigrants, mainly Jews, Greeks and Armenians. In Russia, the social structure consisted of nobles and illiterate peasants or serfs. The peasants were controlled under the serf system, which meant that they could not own land of their own, they were obliged to work on the large estates of the nobles. They were, more or less, slaves.

Ethnic and religious differences, together with economic hardship, have caused tensions, both between the different ethnic groups and with their rulers. These tensions have created a tradition of migration both inside and out of the region which has continued until the last decade of the 20th century.

Political émigrés

There has always been movement of people within and out of Eastern Europe. As early as the 17th century people were emigrating to North America to escape repression at home. Up until the mid-19th century those who moved out of Eastern Europe were mostly political émigrés who would not accept the political systems in their own countries.

Rebels in the Austrian Empire

The Hapsburgs, the rulers of the Austrian Empire, were Roman Catholic and this was to cause problems between them and the countries they ruled where the people were Protestant. In the 17th century, Czech rebels who opposed Hapsburg rule fled to North America. In 1848, the Hungarians also rebelled against their Austrian rulers, but the Russian tsar sent armies to crush the rebellion. The rebels were forced to escape and about 4,000 went to North America.

Poland

Poland, which in the Middles Ages had ruled over what is now Belarus, Lithuania and the Ukraine, was caught between the expanding empires. It was not able to keep its independence. It was partitioned (divided) in the 18th century and there were revolts in the 19th century. During this time thousands of Poles looked for asylum in France, Britain and North America. Some even went to South America.

▲ Fort Ross in California, USA, where Russians grew crops to send up to the trading posts in Alaska.

Alaskan trading posts

As the Russian Empire expanded, Russian explorers and hunters were encouraged by the tsars to chart the unexplored lands that lay to the east of the Ural Mountains. Journeys of discovery ordered by the tsars opened up Siberia and eventually Russian explorers reached the Pacific Ocean. They sailed on to the Aleutian Islands and Alaska, and occcupied them in the name of the tsar.

Russian trading posts were set up in Alaska and California where hunters and native Indians traded the valuable furs from the animals they hunted. Russian Orthodox priests came from Russia to try to convert the Indians to Christianity.

▲ A view of one of the Russian settlements on the Alaskan coast in about 1825.

▼ Catherine the Great (1729-1796), Empress of Russia, who ruled during one of Russia's greatest periods of expansion.

However, the trading posts came to cost more money to run than they generated. Russia was also spending a lot of money in suppressing revolt in Poland and so Alaska was offered to the US government who purchased it for $7,200,000 in 1867.

Immigration into Eastern Europe

There was also a history of people arriving in Eastern Europe from outside. In the 12th century Germans went to Transylvania, now in Romania, to mine its minerals. Germans went to southern Russia at the end of the 18th century at the invitation of the Empress of Russia, Catherine the Great. This early German settlement was to be among the causes of conflict in the 20th century.

Reasons for leaving

From the mid-19th century onwards the situation in Eastern Europe began to change causing people to leave in increasing numbers. Poverty, famines, religious conflicts, lack of land and also of opportunities encouraged not only the poorest people but also those who were moderately comfortably off to leave.

8

Industrial and social changes

During the last half of the 19th century there were three important developments that changed the character of emigration. The first was increased industrialization, both in western Europe and in North America (industrialization came later to Eastern Europe). Countries such as the USA, Canada and Australia had a labour shortage and looked for people from Europe to work in their factories and also in agriculture. The second development was the improvement in methods of transport. Steam ships could travel more quickly than the old-fashioned sailing ships and the development of the steam train meant that by the late 19th century Europe was criss-crossed with railway track.

▲ A team of Russian labourers work on the railways. The improved network of railways over Europe enabled large-scale movement of people.

The third development was the decision taken in 1861 by Tsar Alexander II of Russia to grant the serfs their freedom. This meant that now the peasants were free, in theory, to move, though many were in a lot of debt which kept them where they were. Later in the century, however, more peasants were able to move both within the country and out of it.

▶ Emigrants arrive in the USA by steam ship.

► A Jewish house in Moravia (now part of the Czech Republic) is attacked. Jews were persecuted by individuals as well as by the state.

Persecution of the Jews

Most emigrants left for economic reasons, but there were other reasons for emigrating. The Jews, one of the largest minority groups in the Russian Empire, were subject to discrimination and occasionally to persecution in the form of massacres (pogroms). Jews had lived in the region for centuries but their freedom depended very much upon the whims of the tsar, as did everybody else's in Russia. Anti-Jewish laws dating from 1791 restricted Jews to a particular area, known as the Pale of Settlement, which included Belarus, Poland (then under Russian rule) and the Ukraine.

Different religious customs made the Jews stand out and this made them easy targets for harassment. They acted as estate managers for the nobles and also as moneylenders and these types of job increased their unpopularity. The traditional Jewish respect for scholarship encouraged a level of literacy which tended to be much higher than that of the peasants and this also set them apart.

Settling in North America and Britain

To escape persecution, thousands of Jews chose to join other emigrants leaving for North America at the end of the 19th century. Most emigrants sailed from the large ports of northern Europe such as Hamburg, Bremen, Danzig and Rotterdam. American companies that were short of workers sent agents to these ports to recruit labour. Sometimes peasants were tricked into going to places they didn't want to go to, or into doing work that they did not want to do.

▲ A Jewish scholar in his study. Scholarship and learning were valued and encouraged by Jewish communities.

Bad receptions

Emigrants on their way to North America would often go via Britain, staying there for only a matter of weeks while they waited for a ship to take them on to North America. Many, however, chose to stay in Britain and the numbers of Eastern Europeans, mostly Jewish, rose dramatically, particularly in the Whitechapel area of London's East End which became a focal point for immigrants. They were not received warmly, either by the indigenous English or by German Jewish immigrants who had settled in Britain earlier, in the 1840s and 1850s. There were even attempts by the Jewish press in London to reduce further settlement.

Settling throughout North America

Those who went to North America settled all over the country. They often arrived with little more than the clothes they stood in and had to turn their hand to any work they could find, regardless of whether or not they had previous experience. Clothing, tailoring, boot and shoemaking were popular trades, particularly amongst Jewish arrivals, as were general business and fruit and vegetable selling. The Jews, a more urban people than most other groups, settled in or close to where they had arrived in such cities as Boston, New York and Chicago.

▲ Over the years Jewish immigrants in the East End of London were able to establish a variety of businesses. This photograph, taken in 1954, shows a paper and string merchant in front of his factory.

The Jews in the USA were given more help by the existing German Jewish community (which was larger than it was in Britain) than those who settled in Britain. Research has found that New York Jews were able to improve their situation more quickly than were the Jews of London's East End.

Mining, steelworking and farming were common occupations for other new arrivals in the USA. Peasant farmers were encouraged to settle in the Midwest states of Iowa, Nebraska, Kansas, Oklahoma and Texas. Chicago became the city with the largest Czech population and was jokingly known as 'Czechago'. Hungarians and Slovaks made for the mining areas of West Virginia and Pennsylvania. Many Russians went to farm in Minnesota, Dakota, Kansas and Nebraska. Ukrainians settled on the prairie lands of Canada.

A hard life

Life for the new arrivals, wherever they settled, was usually hard. Immigrants were vulnerable to unscrupulous employers and to dishonest land agents who sold them poor land at inflated prices. They also faced suspicion from other immigrants who had arrived earlier (for example the Irish and Italians) who feared the new immigrants would undercut their wages.

But hardship and isolation were things that immigrants were prepared to endure, particularly if they believed that they would be able to improve the prospects for their children. The words of one immigrant Jewish pedlar in New York describe their hopes:

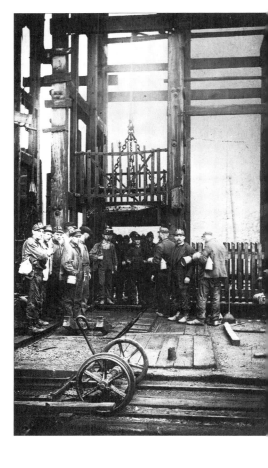

▲ Miners wait to go down the shaft. Many immigrants in the USA found work in the mines.

▼ A settler's farm in the Midwest of the USA. Agricultural work involved a lot of hard physical labour for the immigrant families who chose to take up farming.

'*My boy shall be a lawyer, learned and respected of men. And it is for this that I stand here, sometimes when my feet ache so that I would gladly go and rest. My boy shall have knowledge. He shall go to college.*'

Keeping a sense of identity

The newcomers set up their own communities to protect themselves from the unfamiliar and sometimes hostile environment. In Britain, hostility to Jewish workers from the trades unions led to the formation of Jewish trades unions.

Religion played an important role in helping to maintain their sense of identity. Many social activities revolved around the immigrants' churches and synagogues. In the USA the Polish Roman Catholic Union was established in 1873. In London organizations such as the Poor Jews' Temporary Shelter and the East End Dwelling Company were set up to help with the practical problems of finding accommodation.

Traditional Jewish law required Jews to live within walking distance of a synagogue. This meant that they tended to keep together. Assimilation (becoming part of the new community) was a gradual process for all newcomers, usually associated with economic success and with the weakening of religious ties.

Returning home

It is important to understand, however, that not all those who left intended to leave permanently. Single young men often intended to return home when they had made their fortune. Of the 492,031 Hungarians who emigrated to the USA between 1899 and 1913, 314,547 remigrated. On the other hand, when entire families left it usually meant that they did not plan to return. Young single women did not often go back either. Not surprisingly the Jewish emigrants were usually from these two latter groups.

▲ One of the earliest Polish Roman Catholic churches which acted as a focus for the Polish community in London.

▼ New York has been one of the most popular destinations for Jewish emigrants from Eastern Europe. They have made an enormous contribution to the culture of the city.

Zionism

A small number set up agricultural colonies on their arrival.

▲ The Jordan Valley, which formed an important part of the Jewish homeland in Biblical times. Zionism encouraged a return by the Jews to the lands of their ancestors.

▶ Early Jewish settlers from Eastern Europe in Jerusalem in about 1880.

In 1882 the number of pogroms against Jews in Eastern Europe increased after the assassination of Tsar Alexander II for which the Jews were wrongly blamed. Persecution led some Jews to become active in revolutionary politics. A search for Jewish identity also led to calls for emigration to Palestine rather than to America. The Jewish people were originally from Palestine, but had left during Palestine's occupation by the Romans during the 1st to 4th century.

A Jewish homeland

Between 1882 and 1903 25,000 Jews entered Palestine. A small number of these set up agricultural colonies on their arrival. These settlements were not successful – the harsh climate and land, disease and a sometimes hostile reception from the local Arab communities drove them to the point of abandoning them. They were saved by the financial and moral support of Baron Edmond de Rothschild, a wealthy French Jew. Between 1884 and 1900 he spent $6 million on the purchase of land, training machinery, livestock, and the setting up of schools and medical clinics for the settlers. Farming in Palestine was, nonetheless, a tough business. The Turkish rulers of Palestine imposed restrictions on the sale of land. Financial difficulties and the hard physical life meant that by the end of the 1890s ships arriving at the port of Jaffa were taking back more passengers to Europe than they were disembarking.

In 1897 Dr Theodore Herzl, a Hungarian Jew, founded the Zionist movement, a movement which was to encourage emigration to Palestine by Jews from all over Eastern Europe. This movement was to give an important boost to emigration to Palestine.

Problems in Palestine

The second influx of immigrants from Eastern Europe between 1905 and 1914 saw 30,000 arriving in Palestine. Immigrants were encouraged to learn Hebrew, the ancient language of the Jews. By 1916 a census indicated that 40 per cent of settlers were speaking Hebrew as their first language. In 1917 the British government acknowledged its approval of a Jewish homeland in Palestine and at the end of the First World War took over the administration of Palestine from the Turks.

In the early days of Jewish immigration to Palestine there was little hostility between Arabs and Jews. However, relations between the two communities became worse after the First World War when the numbers of both Jewish and Arab immigrants rose. Riots between Jews and Arabs in the 1920s and 1930s persuaded the British government to restrict Jewish immigration, but the seeds of conflict had already been sown.

▲ Three Jewish men walking near the Western Wall in Jerusalem, one of the important focal points of religious life.

▶ Theodore Herzl (1860-1904) the Hungarian-born founder of Zionism. His vision of a Jewish homeland did not come into being until 1948 when the State of Israel was declared.

War and revolution

The outbreak of the First World War in 1914 caused the flow of emigrants from Central and Eastern Europe to dry up.

At the end of the war in 1918, Germany was defeated and the Austro-Hungarian Empire collapsed. The map of Eastern Europe was redrawn. Poland regained its independence and the Baltic states also achieved theirs. Czechoslovakia was created (by uniting what had been the provinces of Bohemia, Moravia and Slovakia). Hungary, as a defeated state, lost almost three-quarters of its territory and two-thirds of its population. This is why there are now so many ethnic Hungarians living outside its borders in neighbouring countries.

The Russian Revolution

Participation in the First World War against Germany had been a disaster for Russia. The Russian troops were poorly trained and badly organized. In an effort to improve the military situation, all available resources were directed to the army. This meant that the civilian population suffered from food and fuel shortages. The people's anger, which had existed for years, erupted into revolution. In March 1917, Tsar Nicholas II was forced to abdicate and a Republican government was set up. But, this was not the end of the misery for the Russian people. In fact, for many, it was just the beginning.

◄ A procession of priests and workers in Russia. Many different sections of Russian society protested about the power and authority of the Tsar.

Civil War

The moderate members of the Republican government clashed increasingly with the Communists, known as Bolsheviks, who had already established support amongst the workers and army. The Bolsheviks seized power from the Republicans and set up a government with Lenin as its leader. The Russian royal family, by now prisoners of the Bolsheviks, were murdered. In 1918, Russia descended into a civil war between the Communist, or Red, forces and those who opposed them, the White army. This war lasted over three years and caused great suffering.

Emigration of White Russians

In 1921 the Communists defeated the last of the White forces and this resulted in the emigration of White Russians – those who supported the White forces. Many of the White Russians were aristocrats and nobles, but all levels of Russian society were represented in this group. Escape routes out of Russia were often via the cities of Constantinople (now Istanbul) in Turkey and the port of

▲ This cartoon shows Lenin sweeping the monarchy, the church and the capitalists from the face of the world.

▼ Russian refugees awaiting evacuation from Odessa in May 1919 during the civil war. They were helped to escape by the French navy.

▲ The Renault factory outside Paris employed large numbers of Russian émigrés in the 1920s and 1930s.

▼ This fashion plate shows the influence of Russian style on Paris dress design. The men are dressed as Russian Cossacks.

Shanghai in China. These cities were soon crowded with civil war victims and organizations were set up to assist their flight. They could usually travel with only very few possessions. Women from wealthy families often sewed the family jewels into their clothes hoping they would be able to sell them when they reached the West.

White Russians in France

France was preferred to the USA as a place of exile by most White Russians. There were two main reasons for this: first, there was a tradition of speaking French amongst educated Russians, and second, many hoped to be able to return to Russia one day so they wanted to stay as close as possible to their homeland.

Large numbers of Russians were employed by the Renault and Citroën car factories near Paris. It has been estimated that there were up to 3,000 Russian taxi-drivers in Paris during the 1930s. Russian women found jobs in the Parisian dressmaking and fashion industries. Aristocrats, some of whom had never had to work, were now obliged to struggle to make ends meet. They often had menial daytime jobs (a team of dustbin men in Nice was made up almost entirely of Russian aristocrats) but this existence was in sharp contrast to the social life that many continued to lead in their leisure hours, when they attempted to maintain the social life they had left behind.

The close-knit community meant that often Russian could be spoken almost all the time and there were soon two Russian-language daily newspapers in Paris. In contrast to earlier emigrants they considered themselves to be exiles rather than immigrants. Their feelings were expressed by one émigré, '*I had always dreamt of Russia . . . We lived Russia, dreamed Russia, waking and sleeping.*'

The inter-war years

The period between the First and Second World Wars was a time of economic depression and political uncertainty and extremism in Europe and the USA. Inflation soared, workers were laid off and people went hungry. In 1924 the US government restricted the number of immigrants it accepted. Some people in Europe and the USA blamed the foreigners in their countries for the crisis. Jews were used by Adolf Hitler, leader of the German Nazi Party, as a focus for people's fears and frustrations. Hitler promoted a racial theory which grouped people into Aryan and non-Aryan categories. Jews, Slavs and Gypsies were regarded as inferior non-Aryans.

Hitler planned to expand Germany by occupying Eastern Europe. The presence of ethnic Germans in Central and Eastern Europe was used to justify this expansion. The Slavs and Jews of Eastern Europe were to be used as slave labour and then exterminated.

▲ Five thousand Russian émigrés joined the French Foreign Legion. They had to enlist for three consecutive periods of five years to qualify for French nationality.

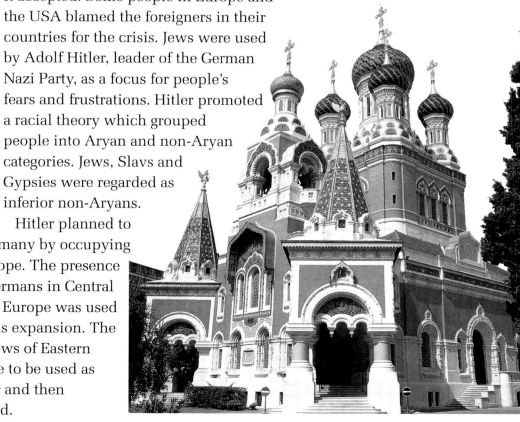

▼ St Nicolas Russian Church, Nice, France. The Russian émigrés built impressive churches in French cities where there was a significant émigré population.

The Second World War

At the end of the war Europe was in a state of complete turmoil.

In August 1939, Joseph Stalin, leader of the Soviet Union, and Hitler agreed to partition (divide) Poland between them. The Soviet Union would acquire eastern Poland and the Baltic states and Germany would get the western part of Poland. Their invasions of Poland in September 1939 marked the start of the Second World War. The alliance between Stalin and Hitler continued until June 1941 when Hitler began his invasion of the Soviet Union. Stalin then changed sides and the Soviet Union fought with the Allies (Britain, France and the USA) against Germany.

Eastern Europeans help the Allies

At the beginning of the war many Polish men were able to escape to the West where they joined the Allied forces. Those in the east of Poland often ended up in Soviet prison camps where they were kept prisoner until

◀ The power of the personality cult ensured that Stalin was idolized by the Russian public. This propaganda poster shows Stalin in a typical pose.

▼ Polish airmen in the Royal Air Force in Great Britain. Poles joined the Allied forces in large numbers.

Germany invaded Russia in 1941. They were then released and Stalin permitted them to form an army under the command of General Wladyslaw Anders. The army was accompanied by a large number of dependants and they were led through the Soviet Union into Persia and India and from there to Palestine and Egypt. Schools and camps were set up for the women and children along the way. From Egypt General Anders and his men joined the Allied attack on Italy in the summer of 1943 and the Polish army fought very bravely, making an important contribution to the Allied success at the Battle of Monte Cassino. Czechs also joined the Allied forces. There was a British Royal Air Force squadron that was composed entirely of Czechs.

Europe at the end of the war

At the end of the war Europe was in a state of complete turmoil. Millions of people had died in the concentration camps where the Nazis sent their political and racial undesirables. Six million Jews were among those who died as a result of Nazi extermination policies. Hundreds of thousands of people had been uprooted during the war. Families had been separated and had no way of locating each other. As late as the 1980s the Red Cross in Poland still operated a bureau for tracing relatives lost during the war.

Concentration camp survivors and those thousands who had been used as slave labour by the Nazis had to be cared for by the Allied armies while arrangements were made to transport them back to their home countries. However, many of these people, known as Displaced Persons or DPs, did not want to return home. Thousands of Jewish survivors of the Nazi concentration camps chose, instead, to settle in Palestine. Between August 1945 and May 1948, 65 refugee boats took almost 70,000 immigrants to Palestine in defiance of British immigration restrictions. In May 1948 Dr Herzl's dream of a Jewish homeland was realized when the State of Israel was declared.

▶ **Children as well as adults were the victims of Nazi concentration camps.**

The Jewish state of Israel has allowed Jews to
continue their cultural and religious life in
comparative peace.
▲ An Israeli boy celebrates his Bar Mitvah –
the Jewish coming-of-age ceremony – in
Jerusalem.
▼ A kosher butcher at work in a supermarket
in Jerusalem.

Settling in Israel

Between 1948 and 1951, 265,000 Jews from Eastern Europe
arrived in Israel. Over 117,000 of these came from
Romania with a further 106,414 from Poland, 18,788 from
Czechoslovakia and 14,324 from Hungary. Only 8,163
came from Russia. For most arrivals, life in Israel began
with a stay in a transit camp. The early camps were
located close to the port of Haifa and immigrants were
accommodated in tents. By early 1951, 17,000 tents in 53
camps housed 97,000 immigrants, both Oriental and
European, one-tenth of the population of Israel. Conditions
were grim. The tents leaked in winter and baked in
summer. Unemployment was a major problem and by 1952
almost 40,000 of the newcomers, disillusioned with the
conditions, had left for Western Europe, North and South
America or the British Commonwealth. Those who stayed
had to accept that hostility from the Arab world would
become part of their lives. Unfortunately the difficulties in
finding a political solution to the territorial disputes have
ensured that relations between Israel and its Arab
neighbours have remained hostile up to the present.

Expulsion of the ethnic Germans

The ethnic Germans, who, as we have already seen (see
page 8), had lived in Central and Eastern Europe for
hundreds of years, were forced to leave their homes in
Poland, Hungary and Czechoslovakia. The decision to
move them was taken by the Allies but the numbers were
far larger than had been anticipated – up to twelve million
were forced to move. Ethnic Germans in Romania were
brutally removed to forced labour in the Soviet Union.

Political fears encourage emigration

Towards the end of the war, while the western Allies
advanced from the west, the Soviet troops had advanced
towards Germany from the east. The political settlement
made between the western Allies and Stalin recognized
that the Soviet Union was to have influence over those

countries in Eastern Europe that it had liberated from German occupation during its advance westwards. It was not yet known how strong a degree of control Stalin would want to take in these countries but many Poles and Czechs and others believed that Stalin would impose Communist regimes in their countries and they refused to return home for that reason. Of the 80,000 Poles who had formed General Anders' army in the West only 310 volunteered to return to Poland at the end of the war. Of the estimated total of 219,000 Polish soldiers abroad at the end of the war less than half (105,000) chose to return to Poland. People of the Baltic states also chose to leave in great numbers. Up to 125,000 Latvians preferred exile rather than to remain under Communist domination and large numbers of Estonians also left their homes, 14,000 alone going to Canada.

▼ This group of Latvian refugees arrived unannounced in May 1949 in Boston harbour, in the USA. They had spent 28 days crossing the Atlantic in a converted fishing boat. They were escaping the newly installed Communist regime in Latvia and sought a new life in the USA.

Decisions for the Poles

Those Poles who chose not to return to Poland at the end of the war had to start a new life. Western governments relaxed their immigration rules and tried to be helpful. The USA and Canada, where there were already large Polish communities, were popular destinations for those who did not want to stay in Britain. Others left for Australia and South America. Australia took an estimated 65,000 Polish refugees between 1948 and 1951.

Settling in Britain

In Britain, organizations both official and semi-official were set up to assist with the care and settlement of the Poles. The Polish Resettlement Act of 1947 set out the areas in which assistance was to be provided, in education, health and financial help. Polish schools and five university faculties had been established during the war. These Polish education centres were gradually closed down after 1945 in order to encourage the absorption of Polish students into the British system. Nursery schools were introduced to teach the children enough English so they could switch to English-speaking schools from the age of five. The Polish community set up Polish Saturday schools so that their children would not forget their cultural heritage. These schools have continued in this role up to the present.

The Polish Resettlement Corps was established to provide ex-soldiers with retraining opportunities and included courses in deep-sea fishing, farming and forestry, and also in building and electrical training. Fortunately there was a general shortage of labour in Britain at that time and most Poles were eventually able to find employment, though the jobs did not always match their previous experience.

Accommodation was a problem and often Poles had to live in primitive conditions in camps that had previously been used by German prisoners of war. This was temporary, but months often stretched into years before

▲ These two girls survived deportation from their native Poland to Russia in 1940 and travelled through Iran and East Africa before finding their way to Britain. Here they are seen in a domestic science lesson at a school set up for Polish refugees near Huntingdon.

people could be moved to better homes. Conditions in post-war Britain, while certainly less harsh than those existing in Eastern Europe at the same time, were nonetheless drab and dreary. One new Polish arrival remarked, *'One thing is sure; any Pole who can learn to more or less put up with the English Sunday will be able to bear almost anything else with ease.'*

The Iron Curtain comes down

In a famous speech given in the USA at Fulton, Missouri, in 1946, Winston Churchill talked of 'an iron curtain' descending between Eastern and Western Europe. This Iron Curtain was to remain for the next 45 years. In 1948, assisted by electoral fraud and intimidation, Communist governments took control throughout Central and Eastern Europe. The Iron Curtain meant that free movement from East to West became almost impossible. The Communist regimes in the East ensured that borders between East and West were heavily guarded and patrolled. Minefields and watchtowers deterred those who considered escaping and border guards were instructed to shoot escapees on sight. The Second World War was over but was followed by a period that came to be known as the Cold War.

▲ During the Cold War, heavily guarded borders meant that attempts made by Eastern Europeans to escape to the West usually ended in tragedy.

The Cold War

Communist regimes in Eastern Europe maintained strict control.

▲ Suspicion between East and West was mutual. These East German guards are closely monitoring the person who took this photograph.

▼ Two of the estimated 200,000 Hungarians who fled into neighbouring Austria after the Soviet invasion in October 1956.

Stalin maintained an iron grip on all the eastern bloc countries. Communist regimes in Eastern Europe maintained strict control through a ruthless and efficient secret police system. People knew that spies were everywhere, even members of their own families could report them to the authorities. Any contact between emigrants and their relatives in Eastern Europe was regarded with deep suspicion by the Communist authorities. The practice of religion was frowned upon and the Orthodox churches were taken under state control. After the death of Stalin in 1953 people in Eastern Europe hoped that there would be an improvement in their situation but this was not to be.

The Hungarian Uprising

In Hungary in October 1956 anger and frustration with the harsh and restrictive regime which had been in place since 1948 bubbled over into revolt. The Hungarians demanded to be treated as an independent country without interference from the Soviet Union. The Soviets pretended to agree to the Hungarian demands but shortly after sent in tanks and soldiers. Within days the uprising was crushed.

Once they realized that their uprising would not succeed, large numbers of Hungarians decided to leave the country. It is estimated that about 200,000 people escaped into neighbouring Austria. From there many made their way to countries in the West that already had Hungarian communities. Approximately 20,000 refugees went to Britain. The Hungarian Relief Fund was set up, and the British public gave what they could.

Czechoslovakia and Poland

The next upheaval in the Eastern bloc occurred twelve years later in 1968. The Soviet Union decided that the reforms of Alexander Dubcek, the leader of Czechoslovakia, were too liberal. Again the Soviet leaders sent in their army. Czechs who were not prepared to stay and live under a regime controlled by Moscow left for the West.

In Poland in 1979 political unrest in the shipyards of Gdansk led to government acceptance of the workers' demands for a free trade union. *Solidarity* was set up in 1980. However, this move was viewed with suspicion by the Soviet Union and the Polish leader General Jarulselski was pressed into outlawing *Solidarity* and declaring martial law. As in the case of Czechoslovakia this resulted in a comparatively small number of educated professional people leaving for the West.

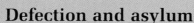

▲ The Polish free trade union *Solidarity* enjoyed enormous popularity.

▼ Soviet bloc tanks rolled into Prague, Czechoslovakia in August 1968 to suppress the movement for greater political freedom.

Defection and asylum

Apart from the periods of political unrest mentioned above, emigration from Central and Eastern Europe during the years of the Cold War was virtually non-existent. Many Jews from the Soviet Union applied to emigrate to Israel but comparatively few were successful. Those who were successful had to make tremendous personal sacrifices as

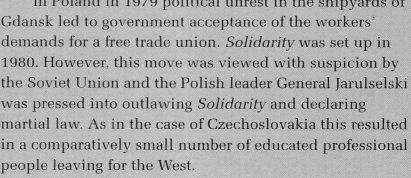

one man explained, '*To receive my exit visa I had to divorce my wife and give up my Soviet citizenship, making it impossible for me to return.*'

Those who were unsuccessful were subject to personal harassment, such as losing their jobs and being watched by the security forces.

▲ The world renowned Russian cellist Miroslav Rostropovich who defected to the West in 1977.

Occasionally individuals managed to defect. Athletes, dancers and musicians who travelled to the West on official trips with their sports teams, dance troupes and orchestras were sometimes able to slip away and demand political asylum from the countries that were hosting their visits.

Glasnost

Changes began, however, when Mikhail Gorbachev became leader of the Soviet Union in 1985. Under his leadership, which emphasized the importance of *Glasnost* (meaning 'openness'), a more open relationship with the West developed and, as part of this relaxation, the number of Soviet Jews permitted to leave the Soviet Union rose. Gorbachev relaxed the Soviet Union's control over Eastern Europe. Economically the Soviet Union could no longer afford to keep Central and Eastern Europe on the tight rein that it had done for the last 50 years.

When it became obvious that the Soviet Union was loosening its control the situation in Eastern Europe changed rapidly and dramatically. Free elections took place and the ruling Communist parties' control was swept away. People voted for democratic government and the capitalist system in the belief that these would bring them the political freedoms and material benefits that they had been without for so long. In 1991 in the Soviet Union, the Communist party lost control. The Iron Curtain had finally been lifted.

▶ Under Mikhail Gorbachev's leadership of the Soviet Union a more relaxed attitude towards emigration developed.

Present day

Immigrant communities have been able to maintain links with their linguistic and cultural origins.

As democracy develops and the economic situation in Eastern Europe improves, fewer people will feel it necessary or desirable to leave there on a permanent basis. The tightening of immigration rules in the West means, however, that emigration from Central and Eastern Europe will never again take place in the huge numbers that occurred in the first half of the 20th century.

Old traditions – new influences

Assimilation over time is bound to weaken feelings of ethnic identity, but immigrant churches and attendance by the children of immigrants at Saturday language schools has helped immigrants to maintain links with their linguistic and cultural origins. Immigrant communities in the West have been able to keep alive traditions that would otherwise have been lost, particularly those connected with religion. It has been noticed that purer Ukrainian is spoken in some immigrant Ukrainian communities in North America than among the more Russian-influenced areas of the Ukraine itself.

A generation is now growing up in Eastern Europe without knowing what it means to live under a repressive regime. Economic reforms have not, so far, brought the material benefits that the ordinary people of Eastern Europe were hoping for. Ironically, now that people are free to visit the West, the financial difficulties facing them make it hard for them to do so. However, many descendants of earlier immigrants can now visit the countries of their origin.

▲ Not all those who settled in the West chose to stay. After the fall of Communism the dissident Russian writer Aleksandr Solzhenitsyn returned to Russia from the USA after twenty years of exile.

▶ Western 'culture' arrived in Eastern Europe very soon after the fall of Communism. In this photograph Russian soldiers queue up at a McDonalds counter in Moscow.

Timeline

c.AD1000 Christianity arrives in Eastern Europe. The Western Slavs were converted by missionaries from Rome and the Eastern Slavs were converted by missionaries from Byzantium.

1240 Sacking of Kiev by the Mongols – Russia remained a Mongol tributary for the next two hundred years.

1526 Hungary defeated and occupied by the Turks after the battle of Mohacs.

1526 Bohemia and Moravia absorbed by the Hapsburgs.

1672 Accession of Peter the Great to the Russian throne. During his reign the territory to the east of the Urals was explored and Alaska was discovered.

1699 The Hapsburgs assist the Hungarians in defeating and ousting the Turks from Hungary.

1791 Poland invaded by Russia and large portions divided between Russia and Prussia. The Pale of Settlement was established. This prescribed areas for Jewish people to live in the Russian Empire.

1794 Attempt by Poland to protect its remaining territory but this attempt was crushed by Russia and Prussia, and Poland ceased to exist as a state.

1831 Unsuccessful Polish revolt for independence from the Austrian Empire.

1846 Another unsuccessful Polish revolt.

1848 Unsuccessful Hungarian rebellion for independence.

1861 Russian serfs granted freedom by Tsar Alexander II.

1867 Russia sells Alaska to the USA.

1882 Assassination of Tsar Alexander II.

1905 First anti-emigration legislation introduced in Britain.

1904-5 Russo-Japanese War. This resulted in territorial rights for the Japanese.

1914 October. Outbreak of First World War – all emigration from Central and Eastern Europe effectively stopped for its duration.

1917 March. Tsar Nicholas II forced to abdicate.

1918 July. Execution of the Tsar and his family at Yekaterinburg.

End of First World War. The map of Europe is redrawn.

1917-21 Civil war engulfs Russia and White Russians flee the country.

1922 Formation of Union of Soviet Socialist Republics (USSR).

1924 USA tightens its immigration policy.

1933 Adolf Hitler comes to power in Germany.

1935 The Nuremberg laws passed in Germany which deprived German Jews of their civil rights (after this thousands of German Jews left Germany voluntarily as refugees).

1938 September. Sudeten border area of Czechoslovakia (where ethnic Germans lived) ceded to Germany as part of the Munich Pact – the terms of which were worked out by Britain, France, Germany and Italy (but not Czechoslovakia) at a conference in Munich.

1939 September. Germany and the Soviet Union attack Poland. Britain and France declare war on Germany.

1941 June. Germany invades Russia.

1945 May. Germany surrenders to the Allied forces.

1945 Borders of Eastern Europe redrawn, Russia takes back eastern area of Poland and to compensate for this Poland absorbs the former German territory of Pomerania and Silesia.

1947-49 Communist take-overs of Eastern European Governments.

1948 The State of Israel established.

1956 October. The Hungarian Uprising takes place – crushed by Soviet forces.

1968 August. Invasion of Czechoslovakia by Soviet bloc forces.

1980 Free trades union Solidarity set up in Gdansk, Poland.

1985 Mikhail Gorbachev elected as General Secretary of the Communist Party of the Soviet Union.

1986 Chernobyl nuclear disaster in the Ukraine.

1989 Gorbachev elected President of the USSR.

1989 Communist regimes in Central and Eastern Europe swept away.

1991 Break-up of the Soviet Union.

Glossary

anti-semitic: against the Jews for no other reason than the fact that they are Jewish. Behaviour or beliefs that harm or discriminate against the Jews are called anti-semitism.

Aryan: a term used by the Nazis to describe people who had their ethnic roots in northern Europe. Some of the immigrants in Northern Europe, for example the Jews, had their ethnic roots elsewhere, even though they had lived in the area for centuries. These people were called non-Aryan by the Nazis. The Nazis believed that Aryans were superior to non-Aryans.

assimilation: process by which person or people of one background or culture becomes part of another culture.

asylum: protection given by a country to refugees from another country who are experiencing harassment.

Bolsheviks: a part of the Russian Social Democratic Workers' Party, which, after the Revolution, adopted the title of Communist Party of the Soviet Union.

capitalism: an economic system where people create money for themselves by owning companies or property.

communism: the theory that society should have no classes and people should not have private property, but goods should be available to all as needed. People who believe in communism oppose the idea of capitalism.

concentration camp: a prison camp where political prisoners, including ethnic minorities, are held.

Cyrillic alphabet: type of alphabet based on Greek but adjusted to the sounds of the Slavonic language. It was devised in the 9th century for a translation of the Bible for use by missionaries among the Slavs. The Cyrillic alphabet is the origin of the present Russian alphabet.

defect: to leave one's country illegally because of disapproval of its political system and to settle in another country which is run under a different system.

Eastern bloc: a group of countries which were under the control of the Soviet Union from 1944-1989, though not part of it.

émigré: someone who has emigrated.

emigration: the process of leaving one's country to settle in another.

ethnic group: a population subgroup of people that share a cultural heritage (language, history, customs etc). An ethnic group is usually part of a larger community.

glasnost: Russian word meaning 'openness', one of Mikhail Gorbachev's main aims in the reforms that he introduced in the last five years of his term in office.

immigration: the process of entering a new country in order to settle there.

indigenous: belonging to a country or region as a native.

martial law: rule by military authority over the civilian (non-military) population. Martial law is usually imposed when civil authority has broken down.

Ottoman Empire: the Turkish Empire that ruled from the 14th century until 1914. At its height, it ruled over parts of Africa, the Middle East and Eastern Europe.

pogrom: an organized persecution and massacre of Jews in Russia in the 19th century which was started or tolerated by the state. Today, the word is used more generally to describe any similar action against a minority group.

Protestantism: a form of Christianity that is different from the Russian Orthodox church and Catholicism.

Republican: the form of government in a Republic. In a Republic, the head of state is elected directly or indirectly by the people.

Russian Orthodox: the main Christian church in Russia and parts of Eastern Europe. It is different from Catholicism and Protestantism.

serf system: a system in which men and women were the property of a landowner who controlled their lives. The system was abolished in Russia in 1861.

Siberia: a region in northern Asia between the Urals and the Pacific. It became controlled more and more by Russia after 1582 and was use for prison settlements.

socialism: a political system which encourages ownership of factories, farms and shops by the people together (rather than by private individuals).

soviet: Russian for 'council'; in the Soviet Union, government was theoretically by councils elected by the people but only members of the Communist Party could stand for election.

Soviet Union: the Union of Soviet Socialist Republics, or the USSR. The Soviet Union covered much of the area that had been the Russian Empire. It was a union of the 15 republics which had formed after the Russian Revolution when some of the ethnic groups within the former Russian Empire had wanted their own nation-state. It was formed in 1922, but broke up into individual republics in 1989.

Tsar: title of the former emperors of Russia.

White Russian: A Russian who supported the Tsar during the Russian Civil War (1918–1921). The term can also be used to describe anyone who was against the Bolsheviks.

Zionism: a movement formerly for establishing, now for supporting, the Jewish national state of Israel.

Index

Numbers in bold indicate illustrations.